W9-BJA-650

131
Boredom Busters
and Creativity Builders
for Kids

Inspire your kids to exercise their
imagination, expand their creativity,
and have an awesome childhood!

Jed Jurchenko

www.CoffeeShopConversations.com

© 2017 by Jed Jurchenko.

All rights reserved.
No part of this book may be reproduced,
stored in a retrieval system or transmitted in
any form or by any means without the prior
written permission of the publisher, except
by a reviewer, who may quote brief passages
in a review distributed through electronic
media or printed in a newspaper, magazine,
or journal.

Printed by CreateSpace,
An Amazon.com Company
Available from Amazon.com

Dedicated to parents, stepparents, foster parents, teachers, mentors, and coaches who tirelessly build into the lives of kids.

Dedicated to the children and tweens who are actively engaging with others, growing their responsibility, and staying creative in an increasingly busy and virtual world.

Dedicated to my own children, Mackenzie, Brooklyn, Addison, and Emmalynn. May your adventuresome spirits, creativity, and love for life continue to grow!

Also by Jed

131 Creative Conversations for Couples

131 Engaging Conversations for Couples

131 Necessary Conversations Before Marriage

131 Conversations That Engage Kids

131 Creative Conversations for Families

131 Stress Busters and Mood Boosters for Kids

131 Conversations for Stepfamily Success

Coffee Shop Conversations: Psychology and the Bible

Coffee Shop Inspirations: Simple Strategies for Building Dynamic Leadership and Relationships

Get Free Books!

Thank you for purchasing this book! I would love to send you a free bonus gift.

Transform from discouraged and burned out to an enthusiastic agent of joy who leads at a higher, happier level! *Be Happier Now* is easy to apply and is perfect for parents, stepparents, mentors, pastors, coaches, and friends.

Discover practical strategies for staying energized so you can encourage and refresh others. This easy-to-read book will guide you each step of the way!

Yes, send me *Be Happier Now!*

Contents

The Power of Play

Although it is only 10:30 a.m., I am exhausted. My wife, Jenny, and I have been awake for most of the night. We are in the hospital's emergency room with Addison, our three-year-old daughter. She has a painful rash that is causing her skin to char and peel.

The bright side is that, after an excruciating night, the medications are finally bringing some relief. Much to my delight, little Addison is in better spirits overall. About an hour ago, a nurse gave her a stuffed baby owlet, which she promptly named after herself. When breakfast arrived, I spoon-fed Addison scrambled eggs and Cheerios. Even with the pain medications, any movement causes her body to throb, preventing Addison from feeding herself.

Soon, Addison, who has a superb imagination, decides that she is an owlet too and begins hooting between bites. It lifts everyone's spirits to see her having fun. This moment of play, in the midst of endless doctors, nurses, and IVs, is refreshing.

Now that breakfast is over, I plant myself in a chair beside Addison's bed, where she has fallen asleep. Sleep is a good sign. According to the doctors, it is when her body will heal itself the fastest.

In the bed to my left, Jenny has also dozed off. This is another positive since she, too, needs to recuperate from the overwhelming stress of this recent turn of events. For me, this moment of stillness is the perfect opportunity to write. Although a hospital stay is an unusual time to begin a book, writing is one way that I manage stress. Putting words on paper is a healing experience. This means that you and I are on this journey together, because helping families heal is one of the many reasons I am writing this book.

Healing Play

As a marriage and family therapist and a former children's pastor, I have witnessed the healing power of play on countless occasions. Just as medical doctors know that sleep is necessary to recover from physical maladies, therapists understand that play promotes healing from past traumas, as well as from the everyday stressors of life. It is how children work through their worries, frustrations, anger, and fear.

Likely, Addison's imitation of an owlet is her way of communicating the helplessness she feels. Adults connect with family and friends in order to talk about their problems. Even when issues are not fully resolved, the simple act of being understood by someone we are bonded with is revitalizing.

Play with Purpose

While adults talk out their troubles, children play out theirs, often returning to the same themes until they find a resolution. This means that play is much more than fun and games. It is a primary way that children heal emotionally, and very serious business.

Unfortunately, as you may have already observed with your own children−or other kids that you know−creative play is gradually becoming a lost art. On the one hand, playing is a natural part of childhood. On the other hand, in our fast-paced, technologically advanced, and highly structured society, creative play is vanishing amid a myriad of activities and digital entertainment options that are more readily available than ever before.

In upcoming chapters, I share insights gleaned from our family's journey from overly scheduled and hyper-entertained to rediscovering the simple joys of life. Then we will dive into 131 boredom busters and creativity builders. These ideas are designed to promote a spirit of active engagement, increased responsibility, and family unity.

Three Types of Activities

Some of the activities in this book will strongly resonate with your family, while others may be less popular. This is precisely why so many options are included. There is no need to implement every idea. Simply select the ones that fit your family's style and culture the best.

This book is about playing with a purpose. Each boredom buster and creativity builder is founded on a key principle. Many of the activities are highly engaging, some promote an increased sense of responsibility, while others do an especially good job of exercising the imagination. A few of the activities fit into all three categories at once. Now let's examine why each of these areas is so important.

Activities that Engage

It was a chilly winter evening, and bedtime was quickly approaching. However, on this particular night, Jenny had something different in mind. After calling our family into the kitchen, where steaming mugs of hot chocolate awaited, she produced a tray filled with hundreds of marshmallows—both large and small—and boxes of brightly colored toothpicks. Jenny enthusiastically announced, "We are going to have a marshmallow-sculpturing contest!"

It is amazing what a family can create out of marshmallows, toothpicks, and a little imagination. It is also astounding how fun this simple project can be. That evening, our kitchen table overflowed with joy as we talked, created, and stuffed our mouths with far too much sugar.

Some of the ideas in this book are included simply because they are fun. These activities are designed to motivate your children to pause their electronics, fully engage in the moment, and build an abundance of happy memories!

Activities That Encourage Responsibility

Over the past twenty years, I have worked with families in a variety of roles, including marriage and family therapist, children's pastor, and camp counselor. As a way of continuing my own growth, I participate in a number of conferences each year. During my early days of family work, I attended a memorable workshop where the speaker homed in on the value of having a family laundry day. The way he described the event made doing laundry together sound like the latest ride at Disneyland. To be honest, it was a little weird.

Fast-forward five years. Life is busier than ever. Although Jenny and I are moving at a rapid pace, we are continuing to fall behind. It feels like we are trapped in a scene from the Star Wars movie, the one where Han Solo and Princess Leah escape down the garbage chute, only to have the walls of the trash compactor slowly close in on them. Laundry and other household chores are piling up, slowly squeezing our family out of our own home.

For some reason, the family laundry story comes to mind. I recall the presenter's preaching on the importance of togetherness, the value of passing on an essential life skill from one generation to the next, and the moments of joy that transpire along the way. Although I have my doubts, we are desperate, and there is one thing that I know with certainty: the laundry is not going to fold itself. So out of desperation, I take the speaker's admonition to heart.

After calling our children into the family room, I dump a pile of freshly washed clothing onto the couch, announcing, "It's family laundry day," with as much enthusiasm as I can muster. Seeing the mountain of clothes, the girls' faces drop.

Initially, there are groans and some dragging of the feet, but ultimately, the sorting and hanging begins. I bring in more laundry, and soon we are folding together. At some point, the stereo is turned on. Heads start bobbing, and the girls sing along. By the time the last garment is placed in its drawer, a full-blown dance party has erupted. Surprisingly, doing the laundry together worked. The clothes are put away, and there are moments of joy in the process. Mission accomplished!

In the spirit of honesty, you should know that our family does not always fold laundry together, and when we do, you will never hear anyone suggest that this is the highlight of their week. Nevertheless, I include this simple illustration because folding laundry is one example of a boredom buster that builds responsibility.

One of our duties as parents is to guide our children toward becoming responsible adults. Simple household chores are one way of accomplishing this. Family responsibilities also help children to internalize the importance of their role within the family unit. In my work with foster families, I suggest assigning daily tasks to everyone in the home because these duties communicate, "Our family is a team where everyone has a crucial role to play."

Permission to Parent Responsibly

Years ago, when that workshop presenter shared his family laundry experiences, I felt like I was granted permission to follow his lead. While parents do not need permission to guide their children to become responsible adults, it helped me to understand that I am not alone on this journey.

As you probably know, parenting comes with an ample amount of guilt attached. Some parents try to offset their overly strict childhoods by being excessively permissive with their children. Foster parents may feel bad about the past pain their foster children endured and overly compensate by doing too much for them.

Stepparents, particularly stepmothers, are also especially vulnerable. Caring stepmoms may shy away from asking their children to help, out of fear of receiving the dreaded label of "evil stepmother" that is propagated in so many fairy tales—think *Cinderella*, *Snow White*, and *Hansel and Gretel*.

In this book, I would like to pass on the same gift that the speaker gave to me. I want to grant you permission to have your children pause their electronics and take on responsibilities at home. Not only will this help your kids grow, but they will also be happier as a result.

In the pages ahead, we will dive into strategies for encouraging increased responsibility in a creative, playful, and none-too-painful manner. As you assign responsibility-building tasks to your children, you may be pleasantly surprised at just how much they are able to accomplish!

Activities That Expand the Imagination

Finally, this book contains activities that expand the imagination. You will find that most of the craft-related activities suggest using items that you already have at home. This is done intentionally, to foster ingenuity.

Do you remember playing with Legos as a kid? If your childhood was similar to mine, then chances are you can recall a time when you wanted a specific piece but could not find it among the masses of other Legos. After sifting through the pieces, you would discover a block that was not an exact fit, but it was close enough, so you made it work. Because the part did not fit perfectly, cunning resourcefulness would kick in. This would lead to new ideas and result in the creation turning out even better than imagined.

The same principle applies to this book. When our children do not have all the materials they desire and are encouraged to figure it out, their creative minds spring into action. The problem-solving capabilities of the human brain are astounding and something that we parents would be wise to encourage.

Employees who think outside the box, and who get the job done under less-than-ideal circumstances, are in high demand. Parents can cultivate these critical-thinking skills early on by expressing confidence that their child can find a solution.

As you can see, engaging, imaginative, and responsibility-building play has plenty of benefits. Play is healing. It advances social skills, grows relationships, and helps our children to succeed in life. The best part is that this is accomplished while our children have loads of fun along the way.

Nevertheless, the transition from overly scheduled and hyper-entertained to a balanced approach—where unstructured free time and imagination are honored—is not always easy. In the next chapter, I share how our family's journey began.

Ingredients of an Awesome Childhood

A soft smile stretches across Jenny's face as she recounts the joys of growing up in a small town in Minnesota. Her parents would order her and her sisters to "Go play outside, and don't come back in until we call for you." Jenny recalls spending hours reading in her favorite tree, swimming in the river that meandered through the far side of her yard, and inventing new dance moves with her friends. Jenny's parents believed that it was safe and healthy for kids to spend plenty of time outdoors, and Jenny has loads of awesome childhood memories because of this.

I, on the other hand, grew up in far different surroundings. My grandfather had moved to the city of Lemon Grove when my dad was a child. During this time, there were an abundance of lemon trees, dairy farms, and wide-open spaces. However, by the time

I was born, the town had expanded to the point that it seamlessly connected to the neighboring communities of San Diego County. Housing developments had consumed the lemon orchards, and a massive concrete lemon was erected as a tribute to what used to be. With a continually expanding population of over three million people, San Diego County feels like one massive city.

Unlike Jenny, my childhood did not include streams, fields, and wide-open spaces. Fortunately, my siblings and I did have a large backyard to explore. Then, as I grew older, the biking adventures began. On weekends, my friend Loren and I would ride for hours. Mt. Helix, a local landmark with an elevation gain of over one thousand feet, was a favorite biking challenge. After doing the strenuous climb, then pausing to catch our breath and enjoy the awe-inspiring view, the two of us would race down at full speed, often overtaking cars in the process.

On other days, the two of us would pedal to the local arcade or to a nearby fabricated lake. Like Jenny, I, too, had many incredible childhood adventures.

An Awesome Foundation

Jenny and I both have fond memories of outdoor freedom, make-believe, and discovery. These ingredients are the highlights of childhood. But don't take my word for it. All of the classic children's stories agree. In the books *Tom Sawyer*, *Anne of Green Gables*, *Alice in Wonderland*, *The Chronicles of Narnia*, and the modern-day *Harry Potter*, the adventures always begin when life is unplanned.

Could you imagine what would have happened if Susan, Peter, Edmund, and Lucy had owned high-tech tablets? There would have been no game of hide-and-seek, no reason to explore the magical wardrobe, and Narnia would have remained undiscovered. In fact, had C.S. Lewis grown up in the twenty-first century, Narnia may have never existed.

In college, I read *Surprised by Joy*, a book where C.S. Lewis reminisces about his youth. He describes the formation of his make-believe animal world, a favorite pastime that laid the foundation for his acclaimed Narnia series.

- Freedom
- Creativity
- Daydreaming
- Messiness
- Adventure
- Friendship
- Boredom
- Problem-solving
- Laughter
- Imagination

These magical ingredients make childhood awesome! Youth is one of the few times when it is perfectly acceptable to color outside of the lines. The downside of a busy childhood is that many of these things are stripped away. I know this because I am a daddy of four girls and have witnessed the disease of busyness invade our own home. Sadly, the hurried life has become so routine that it regularly goes unnoticed.

Examples of increased busyness stretch far and wide. During a recent CPR training, I learned from our health-conscious instructor that while my generation received roughly ten childhood vaccinations, today's children get bombarded with over thirty. When I was in high school, I loved our church's youth group. For this reason, I was saddened to hear our youth pastor confide that he is hesitant to run events because the teenagers in his church are too busy to participate.

Parents no longer face the challenge of finding activities for their kids. The new difficulty is selecting which events they will attend. From healthcare to church, sports, schooling, and leisure activities, there is a never-ending supply of hustle and bustle available.

The bright side is that this does reduce boredom and occasionally makes life easier for us parents—I am sure that I am not the only one who entertains his screaming toddler with his smartphone. The downside is that too much glitz and glamour reduces the need for creativity. This causes me to wonder, *What if all of this stuff is robbing our children of joy?*

Reclaiming Awesome

Our family's journey to reclaiming awesome began a few years ago with a trip to Arizona. After packing up our minivan, we made the five-hour trek to the girls' great-grandparents' home. The drive was an adventure in itself, with the children routinely asking, "Are we there yet?" along the way. When we finally arrived, our girls hastily discovered they had more free time than usual.

The first two days were a difficult transition. Restlessness abounded, and the phrase "I'm bored" was blurted out often. Then, on day three, the magic happened. First, our girls began reading more. So much so that they became lost in their books. Next came socializing with adults and the trying out of new things. Our older daughters learned how to throw a Frisbee with their uncle and baked with their grandma.

Before long, their creativity kicked into high gear. There were art projects, journaling, and dressing up. Our girls even played board games together–a spectacle rarely seen at home. Jenny and I watched with delight as simple childhood joys enveloped our children.

During this trip, I discovered that sometimes the best thing I can do for my kids is to help them slow down. The lazy Arizona days passed far too quickly. We traveled back home, and just as quickly as it had left, the hustle and bustle returned.

There were sporting practices to attend, school assignments to complete, and plenty of screen time. Blaming this nonstop movement on everyone else would be dishonest. Much of the responsibility for this overly rushed pace originated with me. Fortunately, this was only the beginning of our journey. I will fill you in on the rest of the story in the following chapters.

Flexing Creativity at Home

"Daddy, I'm booored." Brooklyn drawls out her words with a mischievous smile. I know exactly what she is doing. Brooklyn is attempting to activate the boredom jar. This brightly colored container, holding nearly one hundred Popsicle sticks, sits strategically on top of our refrigerator. Scrawled on each one is a single activity that encourages our children to flex their creativity. The boredom jar is activated whenever the words "I'm bored" are spoken or whenever our children need a creativity boost.

In our home, the boredom jar is ruthless. Once activated, there is no turning back. A typical scenario plays out like this:

- One of our children utters the words "I'm bored."
- The child who made the offending statement must select a popsicle stick out of the jar.
- The creative assignment is read aloud and the entire house is placed on lockdown until the task is complete.

Jenny and I wish that we didn't have to be so firm, but it is not our decision (at least this is the story that we tell our kids). Until the activity is complete, there is no television, no snack time, and no family games. The assigned task becomes the sole focus, and teamwork amongst siblings is highly encouraged. Brooklyn loves this game. Mackenzie is more apprehensive, yet never fails to engage.

Jenny created the boredom jar a few weeks after our trip to Arizona. To be honest, the jar sat on a shelf for a long time before it was implemented. However, once put into practice, this strategy worked better than imagined–making us wonder why we waited so long. The first time the boredom jar was activated, Jenny and I watched with delight as our two older girls teamed up to create a fantastic Lego city. They had loads of fun in the process.

Our family is learning that creativity–just like any other muscle–must be exercised regularly or it will atrophy. The more our children use their imaginations, the stronger their imaginations become.

Inspiring Creativity at Home

So why don't parents encourage their children to be creative more often? I believe that one of the biggest reasons for this is guilt. Jenny wrote about her struggle with mommy guilt on our blog, where it remains one of the most popular on the site. This is a good indication that Jenny is not alone in her struggle. I know that many dads feel guilty too. Moreover, if you live in a blended family home, as we do, then guilt is even more complicated.

For many years, my two oldest daughters lived with us for only half the week. I would feel bad about the missed time with them and had a tendency to overdo things. I would overload the first half of my week with projects so that I could be more available to them during the second half. I dreaded hearing the words, "Daddy I'm bored," and would rush in like Superman to save the day. However, I have learned that this is not always what is best.

Slowly but surely, I am learning that while children need interactive play with their parents, it is perfectly acceptable for our children to see them hard at work too. Today, I strive to model a more balanced work-hard and then play-hard approach.

Finding Work, Life, and Family Balance

Not long ago, the children and I watched the *Little House on the Prairie* series. The story revolves around the adventures of the Ingalls family raising their children in the 1870s. "Pa," played by Michael Landon, is a loving, hardworking dad, who is often in the fields from sunrise to sunset. This left him little time for hands-on involvement. In the past, many daddies parented with this traditional approach.

I, on the other hand, dove headfirst into the opposite extreme. Feeling guilty over lost time, I strove to take advantage of every second together we had. Today I know balance is best. My children need an active hands-on daddy. They also need to know that both their dad and stepmom work hard to provide for the family.

This means that it is perfectly acceptable to let the children play, and even be bored, while we parents work. This is true for two reasons. First, it is essential for parents to model the value of hard work to their children. Second, free time allows children the opportunity to exercise their imaginations.

The boredom jar is one way that I lay aside my parenting guilt and allow my kids to flex their creativity. In the next chapter, we dive into 131 engaging, creative, responsibility-building strategies. There are numerous ways that you can put these activities into action. You can build your own boredom jar, schedule a regular family activity night, or keep this book handy for whenever your children need a creativity boost.

Most of the activities can be done individually, with siblings and friends, or as a family unit. There is not one correct way to use this book. Now it is time to take action. I wish you and your family much success on your boredom-busting and creativity-building journey!

131
Boredom Busters and Creativity Builders

*There is a garden in every childhood,
an enchanted place where colors are brighter,
the air softer, and the morning more fragrant
than ever again.*

~ Elizabeth Lawrence

*Sweet childish days,
that were as long as twenty days are now.*

~ William Wordsworth, "To a Butterfly"

It is never too late to have a happy childhood.

~ Tom Robbins

Buster & Builder #1

Create your own book of "would you rather" questions. These questions require readers to choose between two difficult and often absurd options. For example, "Would you rather grow a third eye in the middle of your forehead or have a third arm grow out of your belly button?" Then test out your questions on family and friends.

Buster & Builder #2

Have an indoor campout. Set up your camping tent, use art supplies to create an indoor campfire, break out the flashlights, and cook s'mores (15 seconds in the microwave usually does the trick).

Buster & Builder #3

Build the largest and tallest playing card castle that you can.

Buster & Builder #4

Create a catapult from items you have around your home. You can turn this into a contest with friends and family by seeing who can launch a paper ball the farthest.

Buster & Builder #5

Play an indoor game of *Around the World*. Use a wastebasket as your basketball hoop and wadded-up paper for the ball. Select at least five locations at which to stand. Then make your baskets. Keep track of how many shots it takes you to "travel around the world." Then go through the course a second time, trying to beat your high score.

Buster & Builder #6

Write a list of five goals that you want to accomplish in the next year. Then take a small action toward accomplishing one of them.

Buster & Builder #7

Practice juggling. If you already know how, then learn a new juggling trick.

Buster & Builder #8

Juggle a soccer ball by keeping a single ball in the air, using only your feet and knees, for 10 kicks. If you can already do this, try to beat your high score.

Buster & Builder #9

Make a book of conversation starters filled with fun, funny, and creative questions that spark discussion. For example, "If you could have any superpower, what would it be and why?" Bring this book to your next family meal and try out your questions.

Buster & Builder #10

Write a story using this sentence to get you started, "If I were president for a day, three things I would change are..." Then share your story over dinner.

Buster & Builder #11

Make the world's fastest and most colorful paper airplane.

Buster & Builder #12

Plan an un-birthday party for a family member. Then, invite them to the party and celebrate. As a reminder, an un-birthday is any day that does not fall on one's actual birthday. The Mad Hatter and March Hare started this tradition in the book, *Alice in Wonderland*.

Buster & Builder #13

If an un-birthday party is a celebration that falls on any day except one's actual birthday, then an unValentine's is an expression of love that falls on any day except Valentine's Day. Create unValentine's Day cards, or plan an unValentine's Day party, letting important people in your life know how much you care about them.

Buster & Builder #14

Bounce a balloon in the air 100 times without letting it touch the floor. If this is too easy, try it a second time without using your hands.

Buster & Builder #15

Learn a new magic trick. Practice it and demonstrate it to each family member in your home.

Buster & Builder #16

Write a poem about things you like to do. Recite it over tonight's dinner.

Buster & Builder #17

Build an enormous Lego castle. See if you can include every Lego you own.

Buster & Builder #18

Grab your comb, brush, chenille stems, and anything else needed to give yourself a wild and crazy new hairdo.

Buster & Builder #19

Organize a movie night. Create your own movie tickets, make popcorn, and transform your family room into a theatre. For added fun, convert a large cardboard box into a car and make it a drive-in movie.

Buster & Builder #20

Create an obstacle course using items you have in your home. Time yourself going through it. Then go through a second time, trying to beat your previous time.

Buster & Builder #21

Read a book for at least fifteen minutes.

Buster & Builder #22

Make a flip-book, where a stick figure or other objects move as you riffle through the pages.

Buster & Builder #23

Learn to fold a new origami creation.

Buster & Builder #24

Create your own miniature-golf course using items you have around your home.

Buster & Builder #25

Go for a bike ride.

🚲 🚲 🚲

Buster & Builder #26

Practice riding your bike without using your hands.

Buster & Builder #27

Make puppets out of socks or paper bags. Then put on a show.

Buster & Builder #28

Build a sandcastle. Better yet, during winter, transform your garage or basement into a beach paradise. Use your sandbox, plastic kid pool, beach toys, umbrella, space heater, and any other supplies you have. Jenny's dad did this for her when she was a child, and Jenny continues to share this happy memory to this day!

Buster & Builder #29

Play hopscotch. Use sidewalk chalk to create a traditional hopscotch board. Then, after a few games, add boxes to create your own design.

Buster & Builder #30

Prepare for the next American Idol competition. Select your song, practice it, and come prepared to perform at dinner.

Buster & Builder #31

Create an outdoor bowling game using items you have around the home.

Buster & Builder #32

Learn to do a handstand or a cartwheel. If you already know how to do these, then put together a gymnastic routine.

Buster & Builder #33

Get in costume and act out a play. You can recruit friends to help you or do it all yourself.

Buster & Builder #34

Do a puzzle. Then carefully turn the puzzle over and write a secret message on the back. Break the puzzle apart and give it to a friend. He or she will need to complete the puzzle to read your message.

Buster & Builder #35

Use your art supplies to create an original board game. Then teach it to family and friends.

Buster & Builder #36

Play a board game.

Buster & Builder #37

Do mazes or dot-to-dot puzzles. You can find a book you already own or find free printable worksheets online.

Buster & Builder #38

Draw your own book of mazes. For added fun, make copies and time how long it takes each family member to complete them.

Buster & Builder #39

Draw your own book of dot-to-dot puzzles.

Buster & Builder #40

Use your art supplies and items you find around the house to build a boat that floats. Take it to a pond, lake, or bathtub to confirm that it works. For added fun, build sailboats with your family and race them across a kiddie pool.

Buster & Builder #41

Jump rope.

Buster & Builder #42

Swing.

Buster & Builder #43

Make your own joke book filled with your favorite jokes.

Buster & Builder #44

Create an inspirational poster to hang on your wall.

Buster & Builder #45

Create a book listing people and things you are grateful to have in your life. Strive to reach at least 100 reasons you are thankful.

Buster & Builder #46

Create your own knock-knock jokes—the sillier, the better.

Buster & Builder #47

Select a scripture or motivational quote that is meaningful to you and memorize it.

Buster & Builder #48

Make a robot out of your art supplies and other items you no longer use at home.

Buster & Builder #49

Make a nature book that identifies various types of animals, plants, rocks, and insects around your neighborhood.

Buster & Builder #50

Start a garden. If you don't have seeds, make a paper garden using your art supplies.

Buster & Builder #51

Make a treasure map, with clues leading to the treasure.

Buster & Builder #52

Paint with Q-tips instead of brushes.

Buster & Builder #53

Find three toys to donate to charity or someone in need.

Buster & Builder #54

Bake cookies and deliver them to a neighbor.

Buster & Builder #55

Make a list of five things you would like to know about your grandparents, then call and ask.

Buster & Builder #56

Help your parents clean whatever most needs to be cleaned in the home.

Buster & Builder #57

Create a nature art masterpiece. Use your paints, glue, rocks, leaves, flowers, and other objects you find outside.

Buster & Builder #58

Have a thumb war with everyone in your home. Be sure to create a special super-hero costume for your thumb first.

If you carry your childhood with you,
you never become older.
~ Tom Stoppard

Buster & Builder #59

Play a game of tic-tac-toe. For added fun, build a giant board on the carpet. Use masking tape to create the board and paper plates with Xs and Os drawn on the back.

Buster & Builder #60

Design a Frisbee-golf course outside. Then play a game of Frisbee golf.

Buster & Builder #61

Build a lemonade stand and have a sale.

Buster & Builder #62

Make wind chimes using only art supplies and items gathered from around your home.

Buster & Builder #63

Pretend you are a professional reporter and interview a family member. Write out the questions you will ask, conduct your interview, and give a report of what you learned over dinner.

Buster & Builder #64

Make a playdough zoo.

Buster & Builder #65

Send an email to your grandparents. Ask them what they did when they were bored as kids.

Buster & Builder #66

Water the outdoor plants.

Buster & Builder #67

Build a birdhouse using items you already have at home.

Buster & Builder #68

Build a secret fort outdoors.

Buster & Builder #69

Play a game of marbles.

Buster & Builder #70

Play a game of hangman.

Buster & Builder #71

Record a movie on your parent's smartphone and send it to your grandparents. For bonus points, ask your grandparents to send a movie back.

Buster & Builder #72

Create an indoor scavenger hunt with clues to a homemade prize.

Buster & Builder #73

Make your own finger puppets and put on a show.

Buster & Builder #74

Ask a family member what their favorite Bible story is. Then look up the story and read it.

Buster & Builder #75

Put on a lip-sync show that includes all of your favorite songs. For an added challenge, also include your parents' and grandparents' favorite songs.

Buster & Builder #76

Play hackysack with a friend. If you are by yourself, then set a new personal hackysack record for the most touches without the ball falling to the ground.

Buster & Builder #77

Put on a dance show.

Buster & Builder #78

Build a rubber-band shooting range out of Legos, toilet paper tubes, and other items from around your home. Then engage in target practice.

Buster & Builder #79

Write the first chapter of your new book. Then share it with your family over dinner.

Buster & Builder #80

Read a chapter in a nonfiction book that your parents choose for you.

Buster & Builder #81

Read a comic book, or better yet, create your own comic book or comic strip.

Buster & Builder #82

Draw plans depicting how you would like to reorganize your room.

Buster & Builder #83

Create a stuffed animal zoo. Give your family a tour. For bonus points, create an informational brochure and a map.

Buster & Builder #84

Build a kite using only items you already have at home. Be sure to test it.

Buster & Builder #85

Create your own jigsaw puzzle out of construction paper or cardboard.

Buster & Builder #86

Journal about the happiest memory you can recall.

Buster & Builder #87

Have a paper airplane race.

Buster & Builder #88

Make a friendship bracelet and give it to a friend.

Buster & Builder #89

For girls, dress up as Cinderella and sweep the kitchen floors.

Buster & Builder #90

Sweep the patios. Pretend you are an undercover spy, using sweeping as a cover to gather top-secret information.

Buster & Builder #91

Create a favorite fairytale scene in a cardboard box by using your art supplies and toys.

Buster & Builder #92

Practice with a yo-yo and learn a trick.

Buster & Builder #93

Have an indoor snowball fight using crumpled-up newspaper in place of snowballs. Be sure to build your fort first.

Buster & Builder #94

Set the table for dinner. Get extra fancy by making place cards for everyone.

Buster & Builder #95

Create dinner place cards that tell each family member something you like about him or her.

Buster & Builder #96

Look at a cookbook and find something that you would like to learn how to cook. Then make a grocery list of the ingredients you will need.

Buster & Builder #97

Play Jacks.

Buster & Builder #98

Vacuum the family room.

Buster & Builder #99

Listen to a chapter from an audiobook

Buster & Builder #100

Help fold laundry, or better yet, have a family laundry-folding day. Be sure to turn up the music!

Buster & Builder #101

Play store. Create your own play money and items to sell.

Buster & Builder #102

Have an indoor Nerf-gun fight. This is a new family favorite in our home.

Buster & Builder #103

Build an epic sculpture using only marshmallows and toothpicks.

Buster & Builder #104

Offer to do chores for a neighbor who could use an extra hand.

Buster & Builder #105

Practice skipping a bar on the monkey bars. Then see how many you can skip.

Buster & Builder #106

Roller-skate or rollerblade. Learn to skate backward too.

Buster & Builder #107

Create a mosaic out of glue and torn pieces of construction paper.

Buster & Builder #108

Volunteer in the church nursery for a day.

Buster & Builder #109

Create your own address book. Then ask your friends for their addresses so you can add them to your book.

Buster & Builder #110

Create a get-well card and send it to someone you know who is ill.

=▪ =▪ =▪

Buster & Builder #111

Create an "I-miss-you" card and send it to someone you have not seen for a while.

Buster & Builder #112

Create and send a thank-you card to someone you need to thank.

Buster & Builder #113

Make a paper chain. Use it to decorate your room or simply see how long you can make it.

Buster & Builder #114

Look through one of your parents' old photo albums—preferably one before you were born. Then come up with three questions you want to ask your parents based on the pictures in the album.

Buster & Builder #115

Draw the blueprints to a brand new invention. The only requirement is that whatever you design cannot currently exist.

Buster & Builder #116

Turn yourself into a superhero. Create your costume and invent a story about how you use your powers to make the world a better place.

Buster & Builder #117

Write and illustrate a children's book.

Buster & Builder #118

Build an indoor fort out of couch cushions and bed sheets.

Buster & Builder #119

Dip long strands of colorful yarn into Elmer's glue. Carefully add the sticky mess to a piece of construction paper or to an inflated balloon to make a yarn-art masterpiece.

Buster & Builder #120

Create your own sticker book. Use a sheet of wax paper for some of the pages so you can remove and share your stickers.

Buster & Builder #121

Create an indoor bowling alley. Use empty decorated 2-liter pop bottles for the pins and bowl with a soccer ball. Then invite your family to a bowling competition.

Buster & Builder #122

Find and decorate a pet rock. Then make a leash and take your pet for a walk.

Buster & Builder #123

Publish a family newspaper. Report on recent and upcoming family events. Then post your paper on the refrigerator or another high-traffic area in the home.

Childhood is the most beautiful
of all life's seasons.
~Author Unknown

Buster & Builder #124

Have a tea party. Then invite your friends. Real, imaginary, and stuffed animal friends are all welcome.

Buster & Builder #125

Find costumes, dress up in funny clothes, and have a photo shoot.

Buster & Builder #126

Assign everyone in your family a superhero identity. Then draw a picture of how they would look in full superhero attire.

Buster & Builder #127

Build your own piñata. Combine one cup of water and two cups of flour. Mix well. Inflate a balloon, and tear apart thin strips of newspaper. Completely cover the newspaper strips in the water and flour concoction. Place them on the inflated balloon, one at a time, until fully covered. Once this dries, paint your piñata.

Buster & Builder #128

Plan a ten-minute exercise routine consisting of pushups, sit-ups, jumping jacks, and whatever other exercises you want to add. Then put your plan into action.

Buster & Builder #129

Practice hula-hooping or teach yourself a new hula-hoop trick.

Buster & Builder #130

Carve a figurine using a butter knife and a bar of soap.

Buster & Builder #131

Create your own book of boredom busters and creativity builders. Fill it with your creative ideas, and be sure to include plenty of pictures.

Living Creatively

Today, Jenny and I are striving to live what we teach. In June 2017, our family relocated from sunny San Diego, California, to a small town in Minnesota. Initially, the two of us were a little uneasy about how the move would affect our kids. Fortunately, there was no need to fear. Our family has discovered that the slower pace of small-town life suits us well.

Our children refer to our much larger backyard as "the park," and love spending the long, lazy summer days outdoors. Neighbors frequently stop by just to say hi, and when little Addison got sick, they brought treats and let us know that our family was in their prayers. I am also exceedingly happy to report that, after a few days in the hospital, little Addison has fully recovered.

This is not to suggest that life is perfect.

Like all families, we continue to have challenges. Life is, however, remarkably good. While Jenny and I are not anti-television, nor have we declared war on electronics, somehow these things seem less important than ever before.

Both Jenny and I have grown through this process of helping our children rediscover the simple joys of life. Each of us has discovered that a balanced approach is best. I, Jed, have learned that the girls will not die of boredom when the electronics are turned off. I am also learning that I do not need to keep our kids continually entertained. As it turns out, with a little prompting, they are fully capable of having hours upon hours of fun on their own.

Jenny, on the other hand, has eased up when it comes to electronic devices. She is no longer concerned that the occasional television binge will ruin the girls' eyes or that a goofy show will abruptly transform them into mindless zombies. In short, the two of us balance each other out nicely.

Every family is different, and there is no one right way to do things. Each family must decide what works best for their unique style and culture. I hope that the creative ideas in this book, along with our family's own story, are helpful as you and your family navigate this road.

My most significant takeaway from this adventure is a better understanding of just how creative our children can be. I wish you many boredom-busting and highly creative experiences in the days ahead!

Thumbs Up
or Thumbs Down

THANK YOU for purchasing this book!

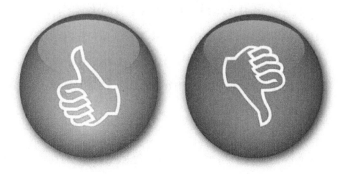

I would love to hear from you! Your feedback not only helps me grow as a writer, but it also helps to get this book into the hands of those who need it most. Online reviews are the biggest ways independent authors–like me–connect with new readers.

If you loved the book, could you please share your experience and leave a review? Leaving feedback is as easy as answering any of these questions:

- What did you enjoy about the book?
- What is your most valuable takeaway or insight?
- What have you done differently—or what will you do differently—because of what you read?
- To whom would you recommend this book?

Of course, I am looking for honest reviews. So, if you have a minute to share your experience, good or bad, please consider leaving your review.

I look forward to hearing from you!

Sincerely,

COFFEE SHOP CONVERSATIONS

About the Author

Jed Jurchenko is a husband, father to four girls, a psychology professor, and a therapist. He supports passionate Christ-followers in leading their families, growing their friendships, and maturing their faith so that they can live joy-filled, Christ-honoring lives.

Jed graduated from Southern California Seminary with a Master of Divinity and returned to complete a second master's degree in psychology. In their free time, Jed and Jenny enjoy walking on the beach, reading, and spending time together as a family.

Continue the Conversation

Let's stay in touch! I always enjoy hearing what others think. Here are some ways to keep connected and continue the conversation:

Blog: http://www.coffeeshopconversations.com/

E-mail: jed@coffeeshopconversations.com

Twitter: @jjurchenko

Facebook: Coffee Shop Conversations

More Family Books

These creative conversation starters will inspire your kids to pause their electronics, grow their social skills, and develop lifelong relationships!

This book is for children and tweens who desire to build face-to-face connections and everyone who wants to help their kids to connect in an increasingly disconnected world. Get your kids talking with this activity book the entire family will enjoy.

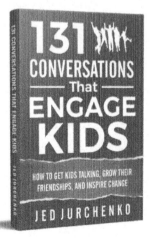

131 Conversations That Engage Kids

More Family Books

Inspire your kids to bust stress and boost their moods as they pursue their goals! This parenting book will guide you on the journey.

Discover:

- Eleven ways kids can boost their moods by changing their thoughts,
- Six strategies that encourage children to express how they feel,
- Five ways kids can elevate their moods through gratitude, and much more!

131 Stress Busters and Mood Boosters for Kids

Made in the USA
Middletown, DE
12 June 2020

97430325R00040